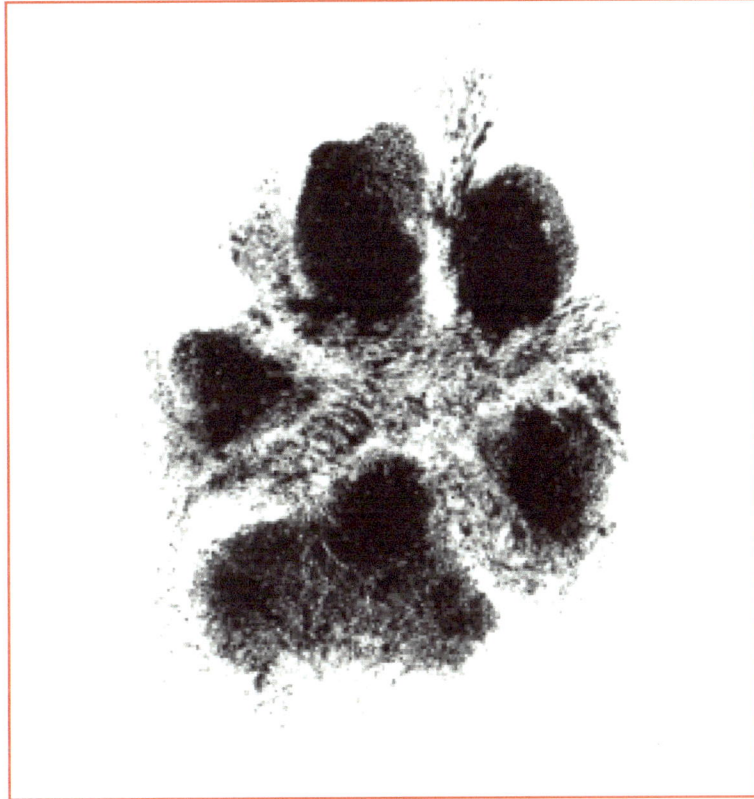

Lucky

Lucky ... Little Guy, BIG Mission 2
Copyright 2020 by Eileen Doyon

Published by Piscataqua Press
32 Daniel St., Portsmouth NH 03801
www.ppressbooks.com
info@piscataquapress.com

ISBN: 978-1-958669-01-3

Printed in the United States of America

LUCKY 2

Little Guy, BIG Mission!

by Eileen Doyon
with Christy Gardner

Illustrated by
Susan Spellman

Christy watches Moxie and Lucky play and thinks, "I will call the veterinarian today to see how they can help Lucky best."

Dr. Jill examines Lucky and takes
X-rays. She explains to Christy
that he has a missing wrist bone.

She feels that removing his leg
from the shoulder would be best
for Lucky. He will adapt quickly
being a puppy.

They set the date.

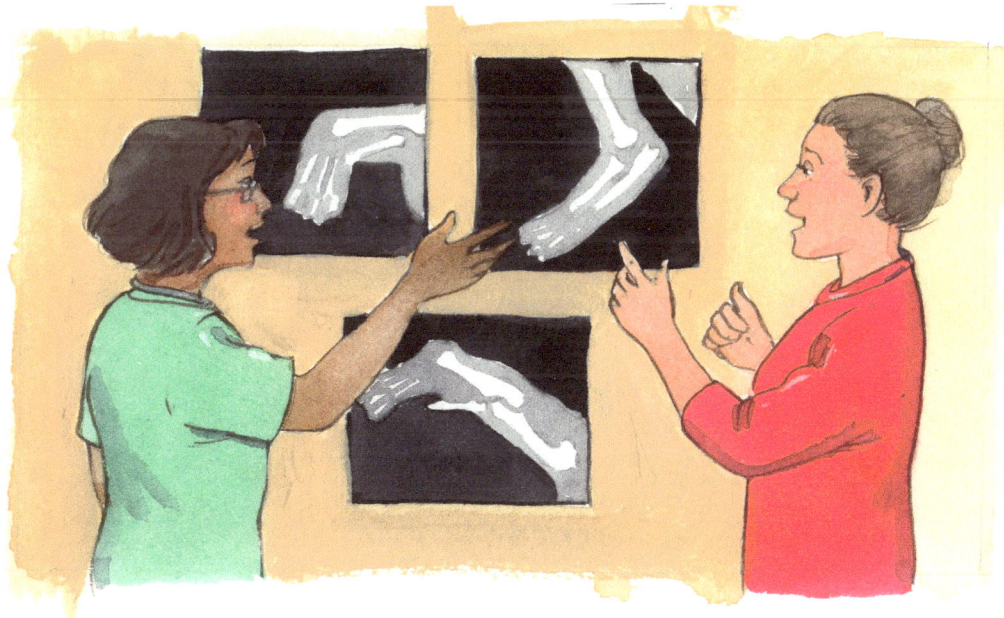

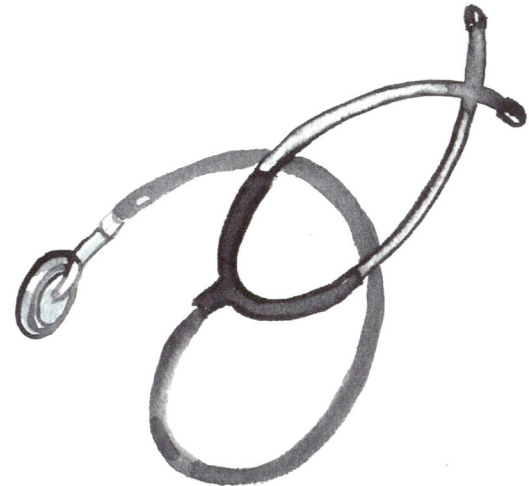

The day comes for Lucky's surgery.
Moxie tells Lucky, "It will be ok. I will take care of you!"

Moxie says, "I love you, Lucky."

Lucky says, "I love you, too, Moxie."

EDOG

Dr. Jill comes out and tells Christy that Lucky did great!

Christy is amazed how quickly Lucky is healing.

He doesn't let anything stop him from playing and keeping up with Moxie.

Lucky dreams of being a therapy dog and does whatever he can to make his dream come true.

Moxie tells him, "You have to work very hard to get something you really want."

Lucky is working on his manners today with Christy.

He tells Moxie that he is tired and finds a place to nap and hides.

Christy says, "How much is that doggie in the window?"

Hehehehehe Lucky laughs.

Christy takes Lucky to Leeds Central School for a visit.

Lucky says, "The kids love me!!! And Moxie too!!! I love training to be a therapy dog. The kids just want to hug me, love on me and give me lots of treats.

I love to play with them
to make them
happy and
laugh."

Lucky flies in an airplane for the very first time and is a little scared.
Moxie tells him, "It will be ok, Lucky. I fly a lot and the people are so nice.
They will give you treats!"

They are off to Philadelphia to visit a school and to make new friends.
They will show the kids how being different is ok.

Someone is watching Lucky and Moxie play.

They say to Christy, "He does well with his disability."

Christy says, "Disability, he does not have a disability. He can do whatever Moxie does. He finds a way!"

Christy and Moxie are traveling for a week.
Claire will be watching Lucky.

She thinks, "How hard can this be?"

She gives Lucky a bath!

Lucky helps Claire with yard work.
He finds a mud hole and rolls and
rolls around in it.

It's so much fun!

Claire is not very happy but laughs,
"Time for another bath!"

Today they are going to a hockey game. The Boston Bruins are playing.

Lucky says, "We got great seats. More kids to love on me and more treats! I love hockey games."

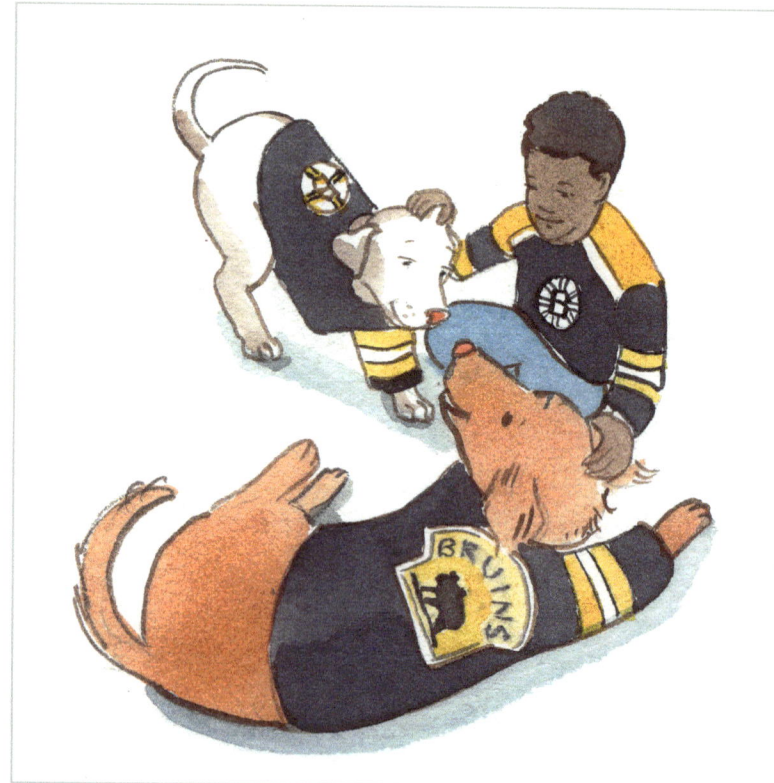

Christy took Lucky and Moxie to New York City in style!

They toured the 9/11 Memorial. A lot of people were hurt there.

They got to eat New York pizza, ride the subway and hang out in Times Square.

Lucky says, "Travel is fun, but I have to work sometimes, too. I ran, well really walked, a 5K road race with Moxie and Christy. We raised money so Christy can help more people have a service dog like Moxie. I got tired and a friend carried me some of the way."

"We got to go swimming afterwards. I can swim just like Moxie, but I always have my life jacket on. I love to swim. We spent the weekend at the lake and had lots of fun."

Lucky wants to be a therapy dog, but still need lots of training.
It's hard work, but he is following his dream.

Christy announces that Lucky is going to be a movie star!

Jennifer at the L/A Community Little Theatre wants him to be "Sandy" in the play Annie. Lucky is so excited, and is meeting all new friends. Christy is training him and Moxie is right by his side.

The headline in the newspaper reads "Lucky, three-legged therapy pup-in-training, cast in Community Little Theater's Annie."

Lucky will be giving out lots of "pawographs."

Christy loves to play sled hockey and always has Moxie by her side with Lucky.
They get to chew on a puck or two at a game. Everyone is so nice.

The big day is here!

Lucky is now officially a Certified Therapy Dog.

Everyone is so happy and Lucky most of all.

With tears of joy in his eyes, he says, "I am so lucky that Christy and Moxie took me into their home, believed in me and made my dream come true.

Now I get to help people in schools and facilities. Dream big and work hard.

I have a new family that will be taking care of me: Claire, Jeff and Julia. I love my new family and my new home!"

Christy was traveling out west with Moxie and received a phone call that a young dog named Doug needed a new home.

Doug was a service dog and helps people like Moxie does. Christy drove to pick him up. He was so happy to meet her and Moxie.

Christy took Doug back home with her. She started training him to take Moxie's place.

Moxie would soon be retiring.

Lucky is visiting with his buddies. Christy tells them, "You are going to be stars in a book!!!"

Lucky shouts, "I am so excited! Wait til everyone sees all of the adorable pictures of me and Moxie!"

The book will be coming out very soon. They will be meeting new friends at book signing events and even have T-Shirts for sale with their picture on the front!

Everyone will want to have one.

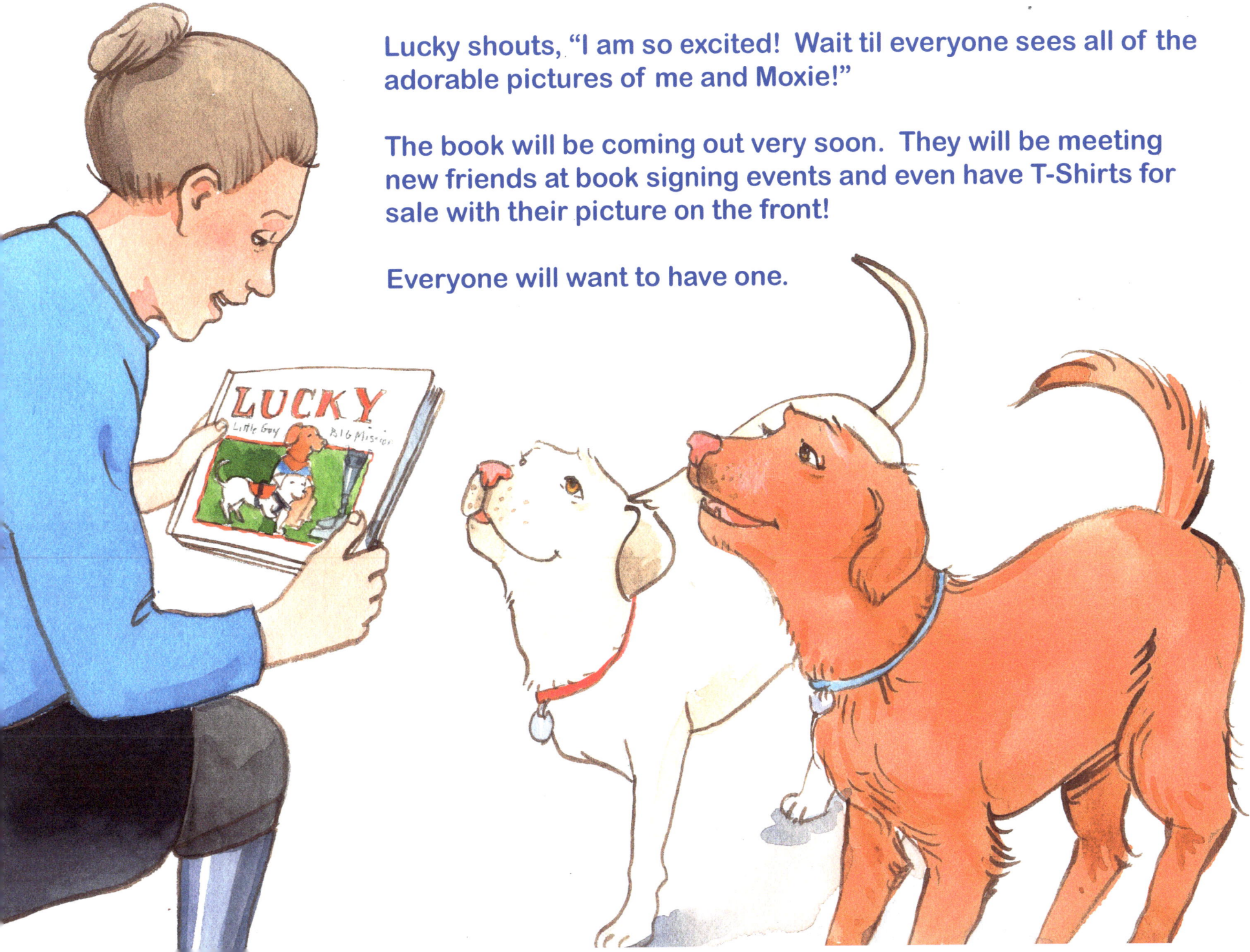

Christy tells Lucky, "I have a dream too. I want to build a place where I can train other puppies to help people. I want others to have a dog like you at school, and like Moxie and Doug to be by their side to help them, and to be best buddies."

Lucky, Moxie and Doug are very happy for Christy.

Lucky says to Moxie and Doug,
"I love being a therapy dog and
helping kids. Just think of all the
people Christy can help."

Lucky is excited about Christy's
new project.

Christy says, "I will name it Mission Working Dogs."

They all wag their tails.

Christy tells them, "We have lots of work to do, so let's get started. Here are my plans."

Lucky, Moxie and Doug all look as Christy shows them what it will look like when it's built.

The name of the street will be Moxie's Place.

They all look at each other and Moxie says, "Here we go again, another adventure!"

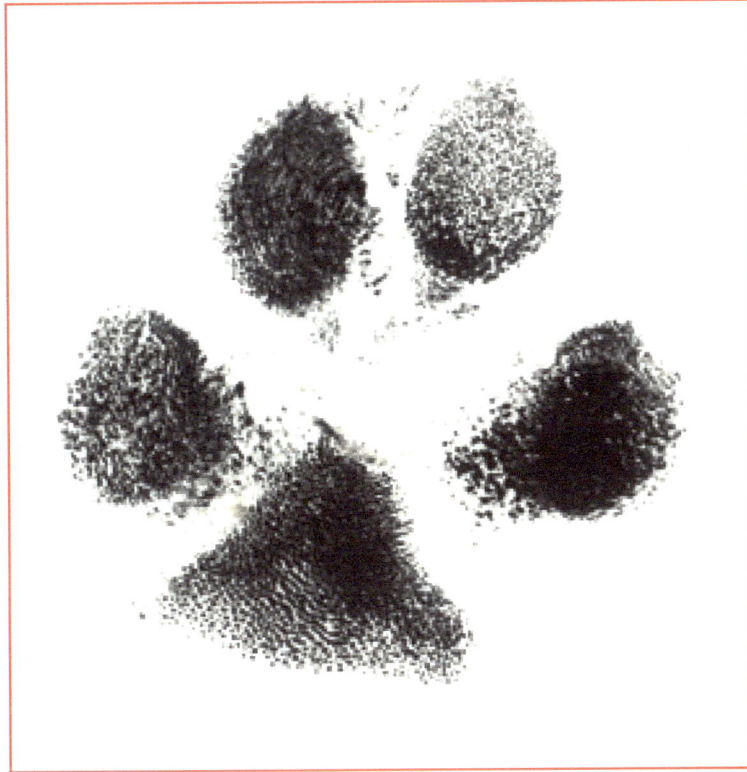

Moxie

In Memory of Matthew R. J. Riley

Matt was an amazing soul. He was fiercely loyal to those he cared about and passionate about only a handful of things: motorcycles, his brother and their family, and his service dog, Gidget, whom Moxie helped train.

Matt served his country in the Army and, despite some struggles, still had some big dreams. While working as a Harley Davidson mechanic, Matt was looking forward to buying his own home and possibly becoming a dog trainer for Mission Working Dogs to train dogs like Gidget to help veterans like himself. Matt wore his emotion on his sleeve, or through his music. If he was singing along to some country you were good to go, but turn around now if you hear some metal playing!

Despite originally getting Doug for Matt, Matt insisted he take over for Moxie so she could retire. Two months later Gidget came into our lives and Moxie and Christy helped train Doug and Gidget together with Matt. Tragically, Matt was killed in a car accident just a month after Doug and Gidget graduated as part of Mission Working Dog's inaugural class.

In Memory of Moxie Gardner

If you read Lucky's first book, you likely know who Moxie was already. Mox was an incredible service dog and more human than dog. It's because of Moxie that Christy got into training working dogs for others in need. Lucky was the tenth puppy the pair trained together before founding Mission Working Dogs in 2020.

As a service dog, Moxie was trained in mobility assistance as well as seizure alert & response. Moxie saw Christy through many surgeries and years of rehab, along with many years of athletics and travel and amazing adventures. She lived a full and incredible life that rivals that of most humans.

She passed away from cancer after a tough battle of surgery and chemo at the ripe old age of 13 years and 8 months.

About Christy

Christina "Christy" Gardner is a 39 year old retired Army veteran from Oxford, Maine. She was injured overseas in 2006 and spent nearly 5 rehabbing before was finally able to live on her own again and started participating in adaptive sports, thanks to her Service Dog Moxie.

She's been on the US Women's Para Ice Hockey Team for 12 years and was an alternate for Tokyo 2020 in shot put and discus. She also represented the USA at the Para Surfing World Championships in 2020.

Gardner has been training service dogs and therapy dogs for the past ten years but wanted to grow that dream to help more Mainers in need. Mission Working Dogs was founded in July 2020 as a local non-profit to do just that. The organization serves to train service dogs and therapy dogs for the local community and has started construction on a new training center in Maine.

About the Author

Eileen has released eight books in her series, *Unforgettable Faces and Stories.* Now with the release of *Lucky 2*, this is her second children's book. Please visit her website www.UnforgettableFacesandStories.com and join her Facebook page, Unforgettable Faces And Stories. Follow her on Twitter @FacesandStories and Instagram @ Eileen Doyon Unforgettable Faces & Stories. Her series was created after her dad's death in 2011 from Lung Cancer.

Eileen grew up in the small town of Fort Edward in upstate New York. She now lives in Portsmouth, New Hampshire along her husband Dan and cat, Otis.

About the Illustrator

Susan Spellman, fine artist and illustrator, started her art career as a staff illustrator at a filmstrip company in Westport CT after getting a BA in art from Marymount College in Tarrytown,NY.

After moving to Newburyport,MA, she began a career as an illustrator of children's books and magazines, illustrating more than 40 books and working for Children's Magazines such as Highlights for Children and Cricket Magazine. Recently, three of the books she has illustrated have won four national and regional awards.

While continuing to work in illustration as a career, Susan also increasingly focused on her interest in fine arts, exhibiting paintings in numerous regional galleries and art organizations throughout the North Shore. She is an avid "Plein Air" painter, a member of The Newburyport Ten Plein Air Painters, and a member of the Newburyport Art Association.

In her illustrations and fine art, a favorite subject has been people, their expressions and movements. Her preferred mediums are oil, watercolor, and drawing mediums.

More information can be found at www.spelllmancollection.com

Thank you to our friends and family for being Sponsors for "Lucky… Little Guy, BIG Mission 2. "

4 Paws and Family Golden Retrievers
221B Tactical - Eliminate the Impossible
Adapt A Vet
Alita and Emma
Mary C Bunnell
Missy Burke
Cochecho Plumbing & Heating
Lee and Millie Collett
Steve, Norma and McKinley Crowell
Theresa Davis
Ella de Jong Change Trainer-Coach
Joan Ells
Bill and Sandy Fisher
Jody and Cheryl Fisher & grandchildren Austin and Mia
Bethany Garboski
Gauthier Home Services
Get Rec'd Therapeutic Services LLC
Gnig
Beth Grauer
Grayson, Tayton and Levi
Gerry and Pam Hamann
Avis Hearon
Holiday Card 4 Our Military Challenge
Jennifer Siller Lasry
Jeremy LeClair
Kathryn Leonard
Dan Libby
Lickee's & Chewy's Candies & Creamery
Loving Hands Creations, LLC
Maine Line Goldens
Maples Crossing
Anita Miles
Kim & Kevin Nace, ASJH
Olivia
Patriot Riders of Maine Chapter 2
Ms. Chloe Plaisted
Posie Mansfield
Christine Ramirez
Rebecca Richardson
Route 1 Barbershop & Shave Parlour

The Salemink Family
Koda Smith
Susan Spellman
Kinsley Spencer
Gail Thomas
Aubrey Troiano
Sienna Troiano
Rebecca Wagner
Kathy Walerius
Cynthia Wallace
Lt. Dennis W. Zilinski II Memorial Fund
Dennis and Marion Zilinski